Swiss Cuisine

The Tastes of the Alpine Paradise

Lukas Prochazka

License Note

No part of this book is permitted to be reproduce in any form or by any means unless a permission is given by its author. All recipes in this book are written only for informative purpose. All readers should be advised to follow the instruction at their own risk.

For more cookbooks please visit
www.amazon.com/author/prochazkacook

Subscribe on Twitter to stay informed:
www.twitter.com/ProchazkaCook

CONTENTS

About Switzerland..6
About Swiss Cuisine..7

Soups

Barley Soup..10
Creamy Onion Soup...12
Chard Soup..14
Cheese Soup...16
Lentil Soup...18
Noodle Soup...20
Potato Soup...22

Main Courses

Älplermagrone, Alpine Macaroni..26
Emmental Apple Rösti..28
Cheese Fondue...30
Chur Meat Pie...32
Malakoffs, Cheese Balls...34
Papet Vaudois, Sausage with Leek..36
Pizokel with Cabbage..38
Pizzoccheri...40
Polenta...42
Raclette..44
Riz Casimir...46
Saffron Risotto...48
Zürcher Geschnetzeltes, Zurich Veal...50

Desserts

Bündner Nusstorte, Walnut Pie...54
Carac, Chocolate Pie..56
Fotzel Slices...58
Chocolate Fondue..60
Meringue..62
Tirggel, Honey Cookies..64
Zopf..66

Volume Conversion...68
Weights of Common Ingredients...69
Temperature Conversion..70
Length Conversion...71

About Switzerland

Switzerland is a small mountainous country located in central Europe. This landlocked country is about the size of New Jersey and is between France and Italy. It is also bordered by Austria, Germany, and Liechtenstein. Most of the population lives in the plateau which is between the high Alps in the south and the Jura mountains in the north. The mountainous area in the south is sparsely populated.

Switzerland is one of the world's wealthiest countries. The Swiss are well known for their watches and clocks. There is not a single official language in Switzerland. People speak one of several languages, including Swiss German, French, and Italian.

The country is made up of 26 cantons or states, which form the confederation. The leader of the government is the president. Both the president and vice president are elected by the Federal Assembly from the Federal Council. They serve a one-year term. Elections are usually held in December. Representatives of the cantons are elected to the assembly for four-year terms.

Switzerland did not become a member of the

Matterhorn, the most iconic Swiss peak

United Nations until 2002, and is not a member of the European Union. Switzerland was formed in 1291 as a union of three states and became an independent country in 1815. The constitution, adopted in 1848, does not allow for troops to be sent to serve in foreign wars. The country has remained neutral in conflicts around the world, including both world wars.

The Swiss Alps are high, snow-covered mountains most of which are over 13,000 feet. The most famous peak is the Matterhorn which is 14,692 feet tall, but the highest peak is Dufourspitze at 15,203 feet. Scientists are concerned that glaciers in the Swiss Alps have lost a lot of ice coverage in the past 40 years. This may be related to global climate change. Rapid melting of the glaciers could cause flooding to the villages below. Most animals in Switzerland live in the mountains. The ibex, a species of mountain goat, was hunted to near extinction in the early 1800s. The species has since been reintroduced and more than 15,000 ibexes now live in the Swiss Alps. Hikers may also encounter chamois, another goat like animal, and marmots. The forests of Switzerland are also home to deer, rabbits, foxes, badgers, squirrels, and many bird species.

Swiss Cuisine

Swiss cuisine combines influences from the German, French and North Italian cuisine. However, it varies greatly from region to region with the language divisions constituting a rough boundary outline. Mind you, many dishes have crossed the local borders and become firm favorites throughout Switzerland. Switzerland owes its rich culinary heritage to its great many regional specialties. Many traditional dishes have their roots in Switzerland's farming culture. Many of Switzerland's national dishes are well-known around the world.

Food, ingredients and the way to prepare it varies greatly all over the country. Generally speaking, basic food items include a huge selection of bread (white, whole wheat etc.), dairy products such as milk, yogurt, butter and - of course - a great variety of the world famous Swiss cheese. Also important are vegetables including beans, carrots, cauliflower, potatoes, spinach etc. Sausages and meat - mainly veal, beef, pork, chicken or turkey - are served in many different ways: grilled, cooked, sliced or cut. Side dishes include French fries, rice, potatoes and different types of pasta. Fruits are available from all over the world, locally grown fruits include apples, pears, grapes and different types of berries, such as black berries, blueberries, raspberries, red currants and strawberries. Finally, there are a lot of sweets, including the second type of food that Switzerland is world famous for.

Switzerland is famous around the world for its chocolate. It owes this renown to the innovative advances of Swiss chocolate makers in the 19th century. Cheese has been produced in Switzerland since time immemorial. The Swiss are also keen cheese eaters. More than 200 varieties of bread are baked in Switzerland. The country is also renowned for its pastries.

Cheese Fondue

Soups

Barley Soup

Yield: 4 servings

Ingredients:

2 tablespoons unsalted butter
2 tablespoons olive oil
1 medium onion, peeled and finely chopped
1 large leek, washed and finely chopped
3 medium carrots, peeled and finely diced
3 stalks celery, finely dice
1 bay leaf
5 ounces smoked bacon, diced
8 cups chicken stock
3/4 cup pearl barley
2 medium russet potatoes, peeled and diced
salt and pepper, to taste
1 cup cream
Fresh parsley, chopped

Directions:

1. Heat butter and olive oil in a soup kettle over medium-high heat.
2. Add onion and leek and cook until they begin to soften, about 10 minutes.
3. Add the carrots, celery, bay leaf and bacon and lower heat to medium. Cook for 10 minutes, stirring occasionally.
4. Add stock, barley and potatoes. Simmer for 1 hour.
5. Add salt and pepper to taste. Stir in cream and bring back to heat, without boiling.
6. Ladle into bowls and garnish with parsley.

11

Creamy Onion Soup

Yield: 4 servings

Ingredients:

7 tablespoons butter, divided
1 1/2 cups cubed day old bread
3 large onions, thinly sliced
1 1/2 cups water
4 1/2 teaspoons chicken bouillon granules
1/4 cup all-purpose flour
1 3/4 cups milk, divided
1 1/2 cups shredded Swiss cheese, divided
Pepper to taste
Fresh minced chives or parsley

Ingredients:

1. Melt 3 tablespoons of butter; toss with bread cubes. Place on a lightly greased baking sheet. Bake at 170°C for 7 minutes; turn and bake 7 minutes longer or until toasted.
2. Meanwhile, in a large saucepan, sauté onions in remaining butter until lightly browned, about 12 minutes.
3. Stir in water and bouillon; bring to a boil. Reduce heat; cover and simmer for 15 minutes.
4. Combine flour and 1/2 cup milk until smooth; gradually stir into onion mixture. Stir in remaining milk. Bring to a boil. boil for 2 minutes, stirring until thickened. Reduce heat to low, stir in 3/4 cup Swiss cheese and pepper.
5. Ladle into four ovenproof bowls; sprinkle with reserved croutons and remaining cheese. Broil 4 in. from the heat until cheese is melted and bubbly.
6. Garnish with chives.

Chard Soup

Yield: 4 servings

Ingredients:

2 bunches Swiss chard
1 teaspoon caraway seeds
1 teaspoon cumin seeds
3 tablespoons extra-virgin olive oil
1 medium onion, finely chopped
2 tablespoons tomato paste
1 tablespoon harissa
4 cloves garlic, finely chopped
6 cups chicken broth
1 lemon, halved
1/4 cup plain yogurt
4 hard-boiled eggs, peeled and quartered
2 cups pita chips, crushed
Kosher salt

Directions:

1. Cut the chard stems into 1/2-inch pieces and the leaves into 1-inch pieces; keep separate. Toast the caraway and cumin seeds in a skillet over medium heat, 1 to 2 minutes.
2. Cool, then grind in a spice grinder or transfer to a resealable plastic bag and crush with a heavy skillet.
3. Heat the olive oil in a large pot over medium heat. Add the chard stems and onion and cook until softened, 5 to 6 minutes.
4. Clear a space in the pan, then add the tomato paste, harissa, garlic and ground spices. Cook 2 minutes, then stir into the vegetables.
5. Add the chard leaves, chicken broth and 1 cup water, bring to a rapid simmer and cook until the chard is tender, about 10 minutes. Squeeze in the juice from 1/2 lemon and season with salt.
6. Mix the yogurt, the juice from the remaining 1/2 lemon and a pinch of salt. Divide the soup among bowls. Add the eggs, pita chips and a dollop of the yogurt mixture; drizzle with olive oil.

Cheese Soup

Yield: 4 servings

Ingredients:

1 tablespoon unsalted butter
1 onion, minced
2 large carrots, finely diced
1 large leek, trimmed, rinsed well, and finely chopped
2 cups vegetable stock
2 1/4 cups milk
2 small white potatoes, peeled and grated
1/3 tightly packed cup thawed frozen spinach
2 cups grated cheese
1/3 cup heavy cream
Salt
Freshly ground black pepper

Directions:

1. In a medium Dutch oven over medium heat, melt the butter. Add the onion and cook, stirring, about 2 minutes.
2. Add the carrot and leek and cook, stirring occasionally, until softened, 4 minutes.
3. Add the stock, bring to a boil. Add the milk and potatoes, and bring to a simmer. Partially cover the pot and let simmer 20–25 minutes.
4. Add the spinach and simmer for 5 minutes.
5. Add the cheese and let melt, about 30 seconds.
6. Stir in the cream. Season with salt and pepper to taste.

Lentil Soup

Yield: 4 servings

Ingredients:

1 tablespoon tomato paste
1 teaspoon dried oregano
1 teaspoon dried thyme
1 cup lentils, picked over and rinsed
1 can diced tomatoes, in juice
2 bunches Swiss chard, stalks cut
Coarse salt and ground pepper
Juice of 1/2 lemon
Bread, for serving

Directions:

1. In a large saucepan with a lid, heat oil over medium-high. Add onion and cook, stirring, until softened and browned, 3 to 5 minutes. Add tomato paste, oregano, and thyme, stir to combine.
2. Add lentils, 5 cups water, and tomatoes with their juice; bring to a boil. Reduce heat and simmer, partially covered, 20 minutes.
3. Add chard stalks and cook until beginning to soften, about 5 minutes. Add chard leaves, season with salt and pepper, and cook until lentils and chard are tender, 15 to 20 minutes.
4. Stir in lemon juice, ladle soup into bowls.
5. Drizzle with olive oil, and serve with bread, if desired.

Noodle Soup

Yield: 6 servings

Ingredients:

1 onion, chopped
2 cloves garlic, minced
2 tablespoons oil
4 stalks celery, chopped
4 carrots, chopped
1/2 small red pepper, chopped
3/4 cup of sweet peas
4 chicken thighs
1l ready to use chicken broth
1l water
1/2 cup small pasta shells
Salt and pepper to taste
Parsley

Directions:

1. Heat the oil in a large pot.
2. Add the onion and garlic and sauté on medium heat until the onion turns translucent. Add the chopped celery and sauté for another 2 minutes.
3. Remove the skins from the chicken thighs. Add the chicken, chicken broth, water, red pepper and carrots to the pot and bring to a boil. Cover and simmer on low heat for an hour.
4. Add the sweet peas and pasta. Remove the chicken thighs from the pot of water. Remove the bone and chop the chicken into small pieces. Add back into the pot.
5. Simmer for an additional 20 minutes until the pasta is cooked through.
6. Add chopped fresh parsley.

Potato Soup

Yield: 4 servings

Ingredients:

5 bacon strips, diced
1 medium onion, chopped
2 cups water
4 medium potatoes, peeled and cubed
1 1/2 teaspoons salt
1/8 teaspoon pepper
1/3 cup all-purpose flour
2 cups milk
1 cup shredded Swiss cheese

Directions:

1. In a large saucepan, cook bacon until crisp; remove to paper towels with a slotted spoon. Drain, reserving 1 tablespoon drippings.
2. Sauté onion in drippings until tender. Add water, potatoes, salt and pepper. Bring to a boil. Reduce heat; simmer, uncovered, for 12 minutes or until potatoes are tender.
3. Combine flour and milk until smooth; gradually stir in potato mixture. Bring to a boil, cook and stir for 2 minutes or until thickened and bubbly.
4. Remove from the heat; stir in cheese until melted. Sprinkle with bacon.

Main Courses

Älplermagrone, Alpine Macaroni

Yield: 6 servings

Ingredients:

500g potatoes, diced
3 cups salt water
250g macaroni
220g heavy cream
1 teaspoon Muscat wine
200g mountain cheese
Black pepper
2 onions, cut in rings
2 tablespoons semolina

Directions:

1. Heat the oven to 100°C
2. Boil potatoes in a saucepan without lid for 5 minutes. Add macaroni and cook them "al dente". Strain and return to pot.
3. Pour cream and Muscat over the potatoes and macaroni, season to taste. Alternating with cheese, place the macaroni in layers into a 2 litre dish.
4. Top with cheese. Bake for approximately 10 minutes in the center of the preheated oven until the cheese has melted.
5. Melt the butter. Mix onions and flour, shake off extra flour. Fry in the butter at medium heat for about 5 minutes until crisp.
6. Place onions on paper towels and keep warm.

Emmental Apple Rösti

Yield: 4 servings

Ingredients:

900g potatoes, peeled and grated
1 tablespoon butter
1/4 teaspoon salt
1 large apple, grated
1 onion, grated
4 eggs, poached or served over-easy
4 slices Emmentaler cheese
Pepper, to taste

Directions:

1. Cover and cook the potatoes in the microwave about 3 ½ minutes, enough to cook them a bit but not make them mushy.
2. Mix together the onions, apple, potato, salt and pepper in a big bowl. Mix well.
3. Melt the butter in a non-stick skillet. Brown the potatoes gently over low heat, turning occasionally.
4. Press the potatoes together to form a flat cake, cover and allow them to continue cooking for about 15 minutes until a golden crust has formed.
5. Turn the rosti onto a plate with the crust on top. You can do this either by putting the serving plate over the skilled and turning it upside down or tossing it like a pancake.

Cheese Fondue

Yield: 6 servings

Ingredients:

200g Swiss cheese, shredded
200g Gruyere cheese, shredded
2 tablespoons cornstarch
1 garlic clove, peeled
1 cup dry white wine
1 tablespoon lemon juice
1 tablespoon cherry brandy, such as kirsch
1/2 teaspoon dry mustard
Pinch nutmeg
Assorted dippers

Directions:

1. In a small bowl, coat the cheeses with cornstarch and set aside. Rub the inside of the ceramic fondue pot with the garlic, then discard.
2. Over medium heat, add the wine and lemon juice and bring to a gentle simmer. Gradually stir the cheese into the simmering liquid.
3. Melting the cheese gradually encourages a smooth fondue. Once smooth, stir in cherry brandy, mustard and nutmeg.
4. Arrange an assortment of bite-sized dipping foods on a lazy Susan around fondue pot. Serve with chunks of French and pumpernickel breads. Some other suggestions are Granny Smith apples and blanched vegetables such as broccoli, cauliflower, carrots and asparagus. Spear with fondue forks or wooden skewers, dip and swirl.

Chur Meat Pie

Yield: 6 servings

Ingredients:

500g shortcrust pastry
30g butter
1 medium onion, coarsely diced
2 slices middle bacon, coarsely chopped
250g beef, minced
250g pork, minced
1 tablespoon flour
60ml hot beef stock
60ml red wine
3/4 teaspoon marjoram
1 teaspoon paprika
Salt, to taste

Directions:

1. Preheat the oven to 190°C. Grease a 23-cm pie tin.
2. Roll out two-thirds of the pastry, and use it to line the pie tin. Bake blind for 7-10 minutes.
3. Melt the butter in a frying pan and fry the onion and bacon over a low heat for 3 minutes. Add the meat and fry until lightly browned.
4. Stir in the flour and add the hot beef stock and then the wine. Stir until smooth and add the salt, marjoram and paprika. Simmer for 5 minutes.
5. Allow to cool and spread over the pastry. Roll the remaining pastry into a lid. Brush the edges with beaten egg and place the lid over the pie.
6. Press the edges to seal and prick the lid with a fork in several places.
7. Bake for about 40 minutes until golden brown.

Malakoffs, Cheese Balls

Yield: 4 servings

Ingredients:

2 tablespoons all-purpose flour
1/4 teaspoon sea salt and ground black pepper
1/8 teaspoon grated nutmeg
400g Swiss Gruyere, grated
2 large eggs

1 small clove garlic, grated
1 tablespoon Kirsch
1 large egg white, beaten
3 cups mild vegetable oil
French cornichons and pickled cocktail onions

Directions:

1. Set a rack in the middle level of the oven and preheat to 165°C.
2. Use a plain 3-inch cutter to cut an even disk from each of the bread slices. Arrange the disks on the prepared pan and bake them until dry but not toasted, about 15 minutes. Cool the bread disks on the pan.
3. For the cheese mixture, stir the flour, salt, pepper, and nutmeg together in a medium mixing bowl. Add the cheese and use your hands, fingers splayed apart, to toss the cheese and flour mixture together until evenly mixed.
4. In another bowl, whisk the eggs, garlic, and Kirsch together and use a rubber spatula to scrape the egg mixture over the cheese and flour. Fold the liquid and cheese together to form a stiff paste.
5. Generously brush one of the bread disks with egg white and place one eighth of the cheese mixture on it. Use a small metal offset spatula to shape the cheese mixture into an even dome. Place back on the pan and repeat with the remaining bread disks and cheese mixture.
6. Let the Malakoffs dry at room temperature for 1 hour. For advance preparation, cover and refrigerate but bring back to room temperature 1 hour before frying.
7. When you are ready to serve the Malakoffs, have heated plates and the pickles and onions ready. Heat the oil in your chosen pan to 350°F, as measured by a deep-fry/candy thermometer. Place 2 or 3 Malakoffs in the oil, bread side down, to seal the cheese to the bread immediately. Fry for 1 minute, then turn over and continue frying until the Malakoffs are a deep golden brown, about 2 minutes longer.
8. Use a slotted spoon or skimmer to flip one so that the bread side is down again and lift it from the oil to the prepared pan to drain for a minute, then serve immediately.
9. Repeat until all the Malakoffs have been fried, serving them with the cornichons and onions as soon as they are ready.

Papet Vaudois, Sausage with Leek

Yield: 4 servings

Ingredients:

1 1/2 tablespoons butter
1 onion
1 garlic clove, chopped
900g leeks, cut lengthwise
30ml vegetable bouillon
30ml white wine
500g potatoes, diced
1/2 teaspoon salt
1/2 fresh ground pepper
300g pork sausage
300g smoked pork sausage

Directions:

1. Melt the butter over low heat and fry the onions, garlic and leeks for 3 minutes.
2. Then add the bouillon, white wine and potatoes, bring to a boil and reduce heat and season with salt and pepper.
3. Place the sausage on top of the vegetables, cover and cook on low heat for 45 minutes.
4. Now remove the lid and boil off some of the liquid.
5. To serve, arrange the vegetables on a warm platter and top with the sausages.

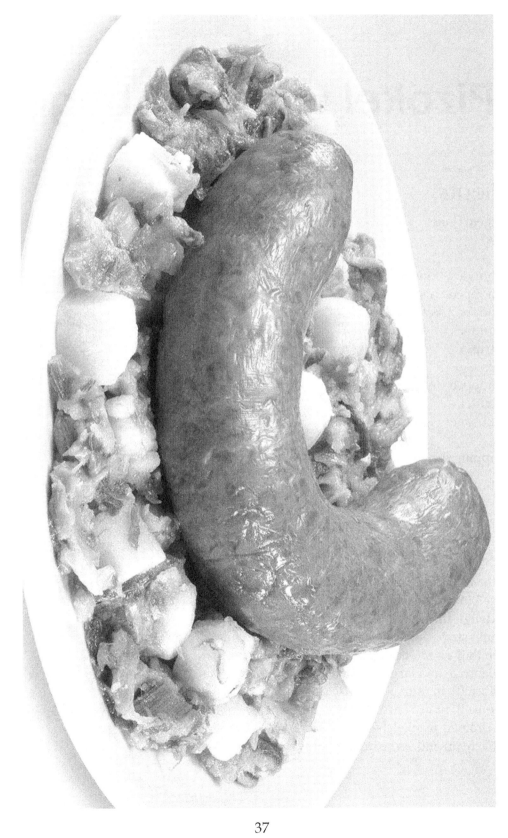

Pizokel with Cabbage

Yield: 4 servings

Ingredients:

220g buckwheat flour
1/4 cup milk
2 beaten eggs
15g finely chopped Bündnerfleisch
15g finely chopped Salsiz
25g finely chopped leek
1 teaspoon butter
60g bacon strips
1 pinch garlic
15g finely chopped onion
1 teaspoon butter
25g Savoy cabbage
25g spinach
1/4 cup whipping cream
Salt
Pepper
Nutmeg

Directions:

1. Put the flour, milk and eggs into a bowl and stir to obtain a smooth dough.
2. Braise Bündnerfleisch, Salsiz and leek in the butter, then mix into the dough. Spread the soft dough thinly over a clean surface, using your hands.
3. Cut into strips about 2 inches long, and drop into boiling water.
4. When they rise to the surface, fish them out with a slotted spoon.
5. Cut cabbage and large spinach leaves into large pieces, but leaving no leaves whole, and cook briefly in salted water.
6. Drain well. Braise bacon strips, garlic and onion in the butter, add vegetable mixture.
7. Add drained pizokel. Season to taste with salt, pepper and nutmeg.
8. Stir in cream and serve immediately.

Pizzoccheri

Yield: 2 servings

Ingredients:

200g buckwheat flour
50g all-purpose flour
125ml water
50g butter
75g freshly grated grana padano
125g freshly grated Valtellina Casera cheese
175g potatoes
200g chard
1 clove garlic
Ground black pepper
Pinch of salt

Directions:

1. Put the buckwheat flour, regular flour, and salt in the bowl of a stand mixer fitted with the paddle attachment.
2. Turn on the stand mixer at medium speed and slowly add the water. Mix until the dough has come together.
3. Remove the paddle attachment and insert the dough hook. Knead for 5 minutes until the dough is smooth and pliable. Cover with plastic wrap and refrigerate for half an hour.
4. Meanwhile, grate the two cheeses, clean and roughly chop the chard, and peel and dice the potatoes.
5. You can roll out the dough with a rolling pin or with a pasta roller. To do it with a pasta roller, take half of the dough, flatten it with your hands, and sprinkle with flour.
6. Run it through the pasta machine at the widest setting. The dough should be 2-3 mm thick.
7. Put the rolled-out dough on a floured work surface. Cut it into pieces of about 8 cm long and about 1 cm wide.
8. The pizzoccheri are now ready to be cooked. Bring a large pot of water to a boil and add salt and potatoes. Also add the chard and boil for 5 minutes. Add the pizzoccheri and boil for another 10 minutes.
9. Meanwhile, melt the butter and allow the garlic to turn brown in the hot butter. Discard the garlic before it burns.
10. Drain the pizzoccheri and vegetables in a colander, reserving some of the cooking water.
11. Add to the garlic-infused butter with the cheese and freshly ground black pepper. Toss to mix over low heat, adding a few tablespoons of the cooking water if needed.
12. Serve on warm plates.

Polenta

Yield: 4 servings

Ingredients:

750ml cold water
170g coarse polenta
125ml thin cream
20g finely grated parmesan
40g butter
Salt
Ground white pepper

Directions:

1. Bring the water to the boil in a large heavy-based saucepan over high heat. Use a wire balloon whisk to stir the water. Gradually add the polenta in a thin steady stream, whisking constantly until all the polenta is incorporated into the water. Don't
2. Reduce heat to low. Simmer, stirring constantly with a wooden spoon, for 10 minutes or until the mixture thickens and the polenta is soft.
3. Remove from heat. Add the cream, parmesan and butter, and stir until well combined. Taste and season with salt and pepper.
4. Serve immediately.

43

Raclette

Yield: 6 servings

Ingredients:

1kg Raclette cheese
Freshly ground black pepper
Cayenne pepper
1kg new potatoes, boiled and kept warm
Cornichons
Silver skin pickled onions
Pickled mushrooms
Salami
Carrot salad:
500g carrots, peeled and grated
1 garlic clove, finely chopped
1 red onion, chopped
1 tablespoon chopped flat leaf parsley
Celeriac salad:
1 celeriac, peeled and grated
1 garlic clove, finely chopped
1 red onion, chopped
1 tablespoon chopped chives
Dressing:
8 tablespoon light olive oil or sunflower oil
2 tablespoon wine vinegar
2 teaspoon Dijon mustard
2 tablespoon mayonnaise, cream or crème fraîche
Sea salt

Directions:

1. Prepare the cheese according to the instructions for your machine.
2. For the carrot and celeriac salads, mix together the ingredients for each salad in large bowls. Whisk together the ingredients for the salad dressing and dress the salads.
3. When you are ready to eat, heat the cheese according to the instructions for your machine.
4. Diners should help themselves to the salads, potatoes and other accompaniments. Once the cheese has melted, scrape it over the potato and add pepper or cayenne pepper if desired.

Riz Casimir

Yield: 4 servings

Ingredients:

2 teaspoons sunflower or canola oil
2 shallots, finely chopped
2 garlic cloves, finely chopped
1 fresh ginger, chopped
4 chicken breasts, sliced into bite-size pieces
100ml white wine
250ml coconut milk
1 tablespoon curry powder
2 teaspoons cornstarch
Salt, to taste
Basmati rice, cooked

Directions:

1. Heat the oil in a large pan over medium-high heat. Sauté the shallots, ginger and garlic for a few minutes until tender and fragrant.
2. Cook the chicken for about 5-10 minutes, stirring frequently, until it's nearly done. Remove from the pan and set-aside. Add the wine and simmer for a few minutes.
3. Add the coconut milk and curry powder to the wine in the pan, and whisk it together until well-incorporated.
4. Whisk in the cornstarch and return the chicken to the pan. Simmer for about 5 minutes more until the sauce thickens slightly.
5. Serve immediately with basmati rice and optional toppings.

Saffron Risotto

Yield: 4 servings

Ingredients:

700ml chicken stock
1 tablespoon vegetable oil
1/2 onion, finely chopped
1 cup Arborio rice
1 cup white wine
Large pinch of saffron
1 tablespoon butter
1/4 cup grated Parmigiano-Reggiano

Directions:

1. Bring stock to a low simmer in a medium pot. Heat oil in a medium saucepan over medium heat for 1 minute.
2. Cook onion until translucent, about 3 minutes. Add rice and a pinch of salt. Sauté until rice is translucent, 1 to 2 minutes.
3. Add wine and saffron; bring to a simmer, stirring, until rice has absorbed most of wine.
4. Add 2 ladles of stock to rice; simmer, stirring, until rice has absorbed most of stock. Continue adding stock, allowing rice to absorb it before adding the next ladleful.
5. Cook until rice is al dente and mixture is a little loose. Stir in butter. Turn off heat. Stir in grated cheese.
6. Cover and let sit 2 minutes.
7. Divide among 4 bowls. Garnish each with cheese shavings, if desired.

Zürcher Geschnetzeltes, Zurich Veal

Yield: 6 servings

Ingredients:

1kg veal cutlets, sliced into strips
3 tablespoons all-purpose flour
60g unsalted butter
2 tablespoons olive oil
1 onion, very finely sliced
2 garlic cloves, finely sliced
15 fresh sage leaves, chopped
220g cremini mushrooms, thickly sliced
1 cup dry white wine
1 1/4 cups heavy cream
Sea salt and ground black pepper

Directions:

1. Sprinkle the flour over the meat and coat well. Heat half of both the butter and oil in a frying pan. As soon as the butter foams, add the meat and brown it very quickly on all sides. Set aside on a plate.
2. Add the rest of the butter and oil to the pan and sauté the onion, garlic and sage for a few minutes, then add the mushrooms. Stir well and when the mushrooms start to soften, continue cooking for about 5 minutes longer.
3. Add the wine to deglaze the bottom of the pan, using a wooden spoon to scrape away any crust that has formed.
4. Add the veal and cook, stirring, until the wine has evaporated. Turn the heat down to low and cook for another 10 minutes.
5. Season with salt and pepper, and at the last moment, add the cream, let it bubble for 2 minutes, then remove from the heat and serve.

Desserts

Bündner Nusstorte, Walnut Pie

Yield: 12 servings

Ingredients:

350g flour
200g butter
200g sugar
1/4 teaspoon salt
1 egg, beaten
Filling:
200g sugar

2 tablespoons water
250g walnuts, coarsely chopped
150ml heavy cream
3 tablespoons honey
1 egg white
1 egg yolk
2 tablespoons heavy cream

Directions:

1. Put all the ingredients for the pastry in a food processor and pulse until homogeneous. With the dough prepare 2 balls and keep in the refrigerator for at least 30 minutes.
2. Put the sugar, water and honey in a large heavy-based saucepan over medium heat. Stir gently to dissolve the sugar. Bring to the boil and let it continue to boil until it becomes a dark golden color. Stir from time to time.
3. Add the nuts and the cream until and stir the walnuts until well coated. Remove the saucepan from the heat and. Set aside to cool.
4. Preheat the oven to 180°C. Grease a 30cm tin.
5. Roll out the larger ball between two sheets of cling film to a 34-cm circle and use it to line the tin of 30 cm square. Press the edges of the pastry against the side of the tin. Scrape the filling onto the pastry.
6. Level the top as well as you can, but don't apply too much pressure, or you may tear the pastry and the filling will leak out. Fold the excess pastry inwards over the filling.
7. Roll the second piece of pastry to a neat 29 cm circle. Moisten the edges of the pastry base in the tin with the egg white and position the second pastry circle on top of this.
8. Use a fork to crimp and seal the edges Mix the reserved egg yolk with 2 tablespoon creams and brush the cover. Prick with a fork in several places.
9. Bake for 35-40 minutes, or until golden brown. Leave to cool until lukewarm in the tin, then loosen the sides, release the clip and carefully transfer the pie to a wire rack to cool completely.

Carac, Chocolate Pie

Yield: 6 servings

Ingredients:

1 cup flour
1/3 cup almond meal
1/2 cup icing sugar
8 tablespoons butter, diced
1 egg yolk
1 tablespoon cold water
1 pinch of salt

Ganache:
220g dark chocolate
4 tablespoons milk
4 tablespoons butter
Icing:
1 cup icing sugar
2 drops green food coloring
2 tablespoons cold water

Directions:

1. Combine flour and butter and mix dough in your stand mixer with the whipping attachment. When the butter is completely absorbed by the flour and has a sandy consistency, add the icing sugar.
2. Attach the flat beater accessory. Add the egg yolk and the cold water, and finally the salt. Mix until the dough becomes compact and smooth.
3. Place the dough on a work surface and press quickly with the palm of the hand. Form a ball and let it rest in the fridge for two hours.
4. Preheat oven to 170°C.
5. Dust the work surface with flour. Spread the dough and prick. Spread dough on tartlet molds.
6. Bake for 15 to 20 minutes.
7. Meanwhile combine milk, chocolate and butter in a small saucepan.
8. Heat over medium heat, stirring gently. Remove from heat as soon as the chocolate has melted and it is smooth. Cool for 15 minutes.
9. Pour the ganache into the baked and cooled tart shells and refrigerate for 2 hours.
10. Combine the powdered sugar, food coloring and water in a bowl.
11. Stir with a spoon until reaching the consistency of a thick ribbon. Do not add water as these proportions will give a perfect icing.
12. Remove the tarts from the fridge.
13. Pour the icing over the chocolate and allow to harden at room temperature for one hour.

Fotzel Slices

Yield: 4 servings

Ingredients:

5 apples, large, peeled and cored
1/3 cup water, cold
2 tablespoons lemon juice
3 tablespoons maple syrup
3 tablespoons sugar
1 1/2 tablespoons cinnamon
12 slices bread
3 tablespoons milk
1/3 cup milk
3 eggs
1/8 teaspoon salt
9 tablespoons butter

Directions:

1. For the apple puree, peel and core the apples and cut into slices. Cook the apple in the water until soft, then mash until smooth.
2. Next add the lemon juice and maple syrup to taste. Sprinkle the 3 tbsps of milk over the bread and set aside.
3. Mix sugar and cinnamon together and also set aside until needed for garnish. Stir the eggs in a bowl and mix in the rest of the milk, add a pinch of salt.
4. Heat butter in a pan and keep warm.
5. Lay the bread slices in the egg and milk mixture to soften them, then transfer them to the heated pan.
6. Fry on both sides until they are golden brown, remove from pan and sprinkle with sugar and cinnamon to taste.
7. Serve apple puree on the side for those who enjoy it.

Chocolate Fondue

Yield: 8 servings

Ingredients:

2 tablespoons sugar
1 cup heavy cream
8 ounces chopped bittersweet chocolate
1 tablespoon butter
1 tablespoon cabernet sauvignon
Pound cake cubes, for dipping
Strawberries, cleaned, for dipping
Biscotti bits, for dipping

Directions:

1. In a microwave-safe bowl, mix the sugar, heavy cream, chocolate, and butter together and microwave for 2 minutes.
2. Take out of microwave and give it a quick whisk. Add wine and whisk again. Transfer to a fondue pot with a flame underneath.
3. Serve with pound cake cubes, strawberries, and biscotti bits on the side, for dipping.

Meringue

Yield: 6 servings

Ingredients:

4 egg whites
1 cup caster sugar
1/2 teaspoon vanilla essence
Pinch of salt

Directions:

1. Preheat oven to 120°C. Line two baking trays with non-stick baking paper.
2. Use an electric mixer to whisk egg whites and salt until soft peaks form. Gradually add sugar, a tablespoon at a time, whisking well between each addition, until sugar dissolves.
3. Once all the sugar has been added, continue to whisk on high for 3 mins. Whisk in the vanilla essence.
4. Use two teaspoons to spoon meringue onto lined trays. Reduce the oven temperature to 90°C.
5. Bake meringues for 1 hour 30 mins.
6. Turn oven off and leave meringues in the oven to cool completely.

Tirggel, Honey Cookies

Yield: 8 servings

Ingredients:

450g honey
100g powdered sugar
1 teaspoon ground cinnamon
1 teaspoon ground cloves
1 teaspoon ground ginger
1 teaspoon ground coriander
1 teaspoon ground anise
1 1/2 tablespoons rosewater
700g all-purpose flour
Oil

Directions:

1. In a double boiler, place honey, powdered sugar, spices and rosewater together. Stir until all of the sugar has dissolved and the honey mixture is thin. Set to the side to cool but not completely.
2. Place flour into a bowl and make a well. Pour the cooled honey into the flour and fold together with a wooden spoon to make a dough.
3. Set the oven to broil.
4. Place the rack on the top shelf. Line one cookie sheet with parchment paper.
5. Roll out portions of the dough on a prepared surface to 2 mm thick or thicker depending on the size of the mold. The cookies will be quite thin.
6. Oil the springerle mold with an oil.
7. Print cookies, cut them out with a cookie cutter, and place them on prepared baking sheets.
8. Broil cookies 2-3 minutes until the relief of the cookie turns golden brown and the underside of the cookies are white.
9. Cookies burn very easily so watch them carefully as they broil.
10. Remove cookies from baking sheet and serve cooled.

Zopf

Yield: 12 servings

Ingredients:

1 package active dry yeast
1 1/3 cups warm milk
1 egg yolk
2 tablespoons butter, softened
3 1/2 cups bread flour
1 egg white
1 tablespoon water

Directions:

1. In a large bowl, dissolve yeast in warm milk. Let stand until creamy, about 10 minutes. Add the egg yolk, butter and 2 cups of bread flour; stir well to combine. Stir in the remaining flour, 1/2 cup at a time, beating well after each addition.
2. When the dough has pulled together, turn it out onto a lightly floured surface and knead until smooth and elastic, about 8 minutes.
3. Divide the dough into 3 equal pieces and roll each piece into a 14-inch-long cylinder. Braid the pieces together and place on a lightly greased baking sheet.
4. Cover with a damp cloth and let rise until doubled in size, about 1 hour. Meanwhile, preheat oven to 220°C.
5. In a small bowl, beat together egg white and water. Brush risen loaf with egg wash and bake in preheated oven for 20 to 25, until golden.

Volume Conversion

Customary Quantity	Metric Equivalent
1 teaspoon	5 ml
1 tablespoon	15ml
1/8 cup	30 ml
1/4 cup	60 ml
1/3 cup	80 ml
1/2 cup	120 ml
2/3 cup	160 ml
3/4 cup	180 ml
1 cup	240 ml
1 1/2 cups	360 ml
2 cups	480 ml
3 cups	720 ml
4 cups	960 ml

Weights of Common Ingredients

Ingredient	1 cup	1/2 cup	2 Tbs
Flour	120 g	70 g	15 g
Sugar	200 g	100 g	25 g
Rice	190 g	100 g	24 g
Macaroni	140 g	70 g	17 g
Butter	240 g	120 g	30 g
Chopped Nuts	150 g	75 g	20 g
Bread Crumbs	150 g	75 g	20 g
Grated Cheese	90 g	45 g	11 g

Temperature Conversion

Fahrenheit	Celsius
250	120
275	140
300	150
325	160
c350	180
375	190
400	200
425	220
450	203

Length Conversion

Inch	cm
0,125	0,32
0,25	0,63
0,5	1,27
1	2,54
2	5,08
5	12,7

Thank you, my reader, for investing time and money to read this book!

The stores all full of many books dedicated to either collecting and sharing recipes or presenting the new ones. I sincerely thank you for choosing this very book and reading it to its very end.

I hope you have enjoyed this book as much as possible and that you have learnt something new and interesting. If you have enjoyed this book, please take a few minutes to write a review summarizing your thoughts and opinion on this book.

If you are interested in other books of mine check out my official amazon author's profile:

www.amazon.com/author/prochazkacook

Thanks for buying this book and have best of luck.

Sincerely,

Lukas Prochazka

Learn more about cuisines of the world

If you are interested in other cookbook you should consider checking out these honourable mentions.

Vietnam is a country with rich background culture. In the last century Vietnam has experienced a turmoil that led to the spreading of Vietnamese culture all around the world. Most of these immigrants ended up in Europe especially in Czech Republic, where they make the biggest minority. In this book, you will find genuine recipes from Vietnam.

Austria was once a great empire. It was a melting pot of dozens of cultures standing under one flag and under one leader. In its capital city of Vienna, the best of each part combined to make one of the best cuisines of all the world.

Germany is a country with large historical and cultural heritage. Once it was a group of dozens small states fighting each other. Later the Germany went through on of the worst events history remembers. However, the German culture stands unbroken. Learn more about the culture of one of the world defining countries.

Made in the USA
Columbia, SC
20 December 2019